IRISH RAILWAYS
in the heyday of steam

other titles by H. C. CASSERLEY in this pictorial series include

LNER STEAM 1923–1948

LNER LOCOMOTIVES 1923–1948

LMSR STEAM 1923–1948

LMSR LOCOMOTIVES 1923–1948 [three volumes]

LIGHT RAILWAYS OF BRITAIN

THE LATER YEARS OF METROPOLITAN STEAM

SCOTTISH RAILWAYS IN THE HEYDAY OF STEAM

WELSH RAILWAYS IN THE HEYDAY OF STEAM

IRISH RAILWAYS

in the heyday of steam

H. C. CASSERLEY

D. BRADFORD BARTON LTD

Inchicore shed on 24 April 1955—towards the end of the heyday of steam on Irish railways.   [R.M. Casserley]

Published by Roberts Wholesale Books Limited
Unit 12, Benson Street Enterprise Centre, Hanover Quay, Dublin 2

Printed and bound in Great Britain by BPC Hazell Books Ltd

introduction

The 'Heyday of Steam' on most of the world's railway systems can be said to have been the period between the two World Wars and the few years after the termination of the second of these conflicts, - that is, from 1945 to the early 1950s. This is certainly true of Great Britain and Ireland, in which countries the development of the steam locomotive had proceeded on roughly similar lines, although, in the case of Ireland, lagging something like twenty years behind. This is well exemplified by the fact that whereas on the major British railways (with the exception of the G.W.R.) the ultimate progress in express locomotive design had developed from the 4-4-0 to the Pacific, in Ireland the 4-4-0 remained the principal passenger type. In fact as few as 22 4-6-0s ever ran in that country, whilst eight-coupled engines totalled in all a modest six - heavy goods locomotives being unknown as there was no mineral traffic of such a nature as to require it. The ubiquitous 0-6-0 held its own to the end as the general all-purpose type of engine.

The result was that Ireland was a paradise for the connoisseur during the 1920s and 1930s, when one could encounter a variety of railway scenes more remindful of the colourful Edwardian years before the onset of large locomotives and standardisation.

In speaking of Ireland, although the South is in fact a foreign country, one still thinks of it as one entity from a railway point of view, as it was before the 'troubles'; these started with the 1916 rebellion, leading to the partition of the country in 1921 and the secession of the South from the Commonwealth with the creation of the Irish Free State, known as Eire, or more currently referred to as the Irish Republic.

Allowing for the time lag already referred to, the development and style of English and Irish locomotives followed a very similar pattern, retaining their neat and handsome, uniquely British outlines, never to be disfigured by the stark ugliness which was to be found abroad, particularly on most European and American railways.

There were marked similarities between some of the English and Irish companies, partly due so far as the engines were concerned to the fact that there was a certain amount of transfer of locomotive superintendents from one country to the other. The Belfast & Northern Counties had moreover been taken over by the Midland Railway of England and consequently became virtually a miniature edition of that enterprising concern, and later to become part of the L.M.S. system.

Other events concerning the railways in general also followed various similarities. In 1925 all companies lying entirely within the Free State were compulsorily amalgamated into one entity, the Great Southern Railways, much on the lines of the English groupings of 1923, but as a single body instead of four groups. This became Coras Iompair Eireann (Irish Transport Company) in 1945, which embraced all forms of transport, including rail, road and canals. It was finally nationalised in 1950, following the example of the creation of British Railways in 1948.

In the North, the remaining lines continued their independence until the formation of the Ulster Transport Authority in 1948, but the Northern Ireland Government showed a strong anti-rail bias in favour of road transport, and proceeded with drastic closures, so that little of the once-extensive rail network now remains. The north west of the country, the whole of Donegal and much of the counties of Londonderry, Fermanagh and Leitrim, are today entirely without rail facilities.

The Great Northern, together with a few small lines which lay partly in the Free State and partly in Northern Ireland, had not been involved in the 1925 amalgamation, and continued to operate independently. The G.N.R., in some ways the most important in the country, linking as it did the two principal cities, Dublin and Belfast, was a very efficient and progressive concern until it fell on bad times in the early 1950s, and was for a time operated on a joint basis with financial support from the governments of both countries, as the Great Northern Railway Board. This was dissolved in 1958 and the system divided between the C.I.E. and U.T.A., the locomotive stock being apportioned equally between the two concerns.

In spite of the slow disappearance of steam power over the years, when it came to eventual dieselisation the changeover was carried into effect more rapidly than on British Railways. This was possible because of the enormous difference in size of the respective systems and the much smaller number of new engines needed. To give a very rough idea, there were in the late 1950s about 700 locomotives necessary to operate the whole of the Irish railway system, compared with something in the region of 20,000 in Great Britain.

The first main line diesel locomotives appeared in 1955, and by 1965 the steam locomotive had virtually disappeared in the Irish Republic, three years ahead of British Railways. A few N.C.C. 2-6-4Ts survived in working order in Northern Ireland until 1970. The modern multiple unit diesel railcars had been introduced by the Great Northern in 1950, anticipating the large fleet which now forms such a considerable part of the British railway scene.

It is now difficult to imagine that until that time almost every train operating in the whole of Ireland, with a few small exceptions such as the Drumm battery cars on the Dublin suburban service, a few single unit diesel railcars here and there, mainly in the north, and two minor electric lines of ancient origin (The Bessbrook & Newry, and Giant's Causeway, closed in 1948/9) was steam operated. This is the scene which this album seeks to portray.

I have been able to illustrate it almost entirely by my own photographs, taken on about a dozen or so lengthy explorations of the Emerald Isle between 1929 and 1955, together with a few by my son, who accompanied me on the later ones between 1948 and 1955, and on his own in 1961. Later visits proved an anti-climax for what steam still remained in the final years was in a dirty or derelict condition - apart from a few excellent and enjoyable rail tours, well illustrated at the time—so that few photographs of the final period are worthy of inclusion.

H. C. CASSERLEY

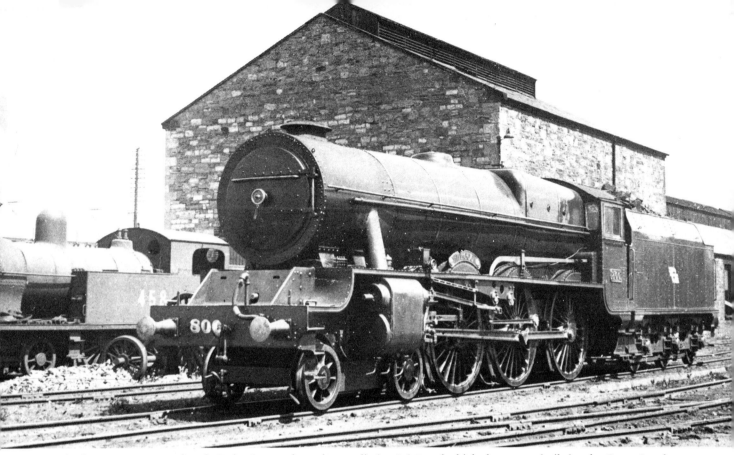

The largest express engines in Ireland were these three cylinder 4-6-0s, of which three were built by the Great Southern Railways at Inchicore in 1939 for Dublin-Cork expresses. They were destined to be the last steam locomotives for C.I.E., if one discounts Bulleid's experimental turf burner of 1957. No.800 is at Inchicore on 16 May 1950 with the new C.I.E. emblem on the tender. The strong resemblance to a rebuilt 'Royal Scot' of the L.M.S. will be noted, the first example of which had appeared in 1935 in the form of No.6170 *British Legion*, a conversion of the ill-fated high pressure engine *Fury*.

Naming of locomotives had been very rare on the G.S.R, but some locomotives were honoured by commemorating former Queens of Ireland, in Erse lettering; No.800 *Maeve*, No.801 *Macha*, No.802 *Tailte*, No.800 is preserved in Belfast Museum. They were also painted green, departing from the long established black or grey which had been the practice over a period of many years.

An earlier class of four-cylinder 4-6-0s for the main line of the G.S. & W.R. first appeared in 1916 (No.400), followed by nine others in 1921 (Nos.401-409). Most of them were later rebuilt with two cylinders, a couple of them with Caprotti valve gear. No.409, in original condition, is seen here entering Limerick Junction on 16 September 1929 with a Cork – Dublin express.

Limerick Junction, was a well known Irish railway oddity—an important interchange point between the Dublin-Cork and Waterford-Limerick main lines, which crossed on the level at approximate right angles. Situated in open country, its outstanding peculiarity was that all trains had to reverse into their respective platforms, the two main line engines facing each other, as E.L. Ahrons once put it, 'like a couple of Kilkenny cats' (nowadays these trains have a straight run-in, but otherwise the same arrangement still applies to the Limerick & Waterford trains). This view, taken on 11 July 1932, shows 4-4-0 No.312 with a stopping train to Dublin, and No.405 with a full head of steam blowing off vigorously and about to leave with a Cork express.

Between 1950 and 1953 the 'Enterprise Express', the G.N.R. crack train between Belfast and Dublin, ran by mutual agreement with C.I.E. through between Belfast and Cork, calling at the Great Northern station at Amiens Street where the train reversed with change of engine from G.N.R. to C.I.E., and by-passing the Great Southern terminal at Kingsbridge. It is seen here passing Inchicore on 24 April 1953 with Caprotti fitted 4-6-0 No.406.

Inside cylinder 2-6-0 No.360, one of a series of seven engines built in 1903 as 0-6-0s and later modified by the addition of a pony truck, near Inchicore on 16 April 1948, was photographed during the period of an acute coal shortage. Ireland has no natural supplies of any consequence of its own which partly accounted for the rapid change over to dieselisation and a number of engines were converted to oil burning. For easy identification, these were painted with large white circles on the smoke box and tender.

In 1925 the G.S.R. purchased a number of parts of 2-6-0s of Maunsell's S.E. & C.R. design, which had been built at Woolwich in 1920-21. R.E.L. Maunsell was in fact loco superintendent of the G.S. & W.R. from 1911 to 1913, and it is curious that engines of his design should have appeared on the Great Southern after he had been with the Southern Railway in England for many years. Except for the gauge of 5′ 3″ instead of 4′ 8½″ they were virtually identical with their S.R. counterparts, Class N. The G.S.R. engines were Nos.372-391; No.386 is seen here leaving Limerick Junction on 30 June 1938 with a Cork express.

A later view of one of these engines (which it was never found necessary to fit with smokebox steam deflectors as on the S.R.) at Mullingar on 15 April 1948 with a tender brimming over after replenishing the water supply. G.S. & W.R. number plates of unmistakable Crewe ancestry had gradually been replaced during the war years by painted numbers and also smokebox door number plates were fitted, L.M.S. and B.R. style, as depicted in other illustrations (e.g. page 11).

Some of these Woolwich built parts were provided with 6′ 0″ driving wheels (thus corresponding to Class U on the S.R. of England). This lot, Nos.393-398, were assembled at Inchicore in 1930. They worked principally on the main M.G.W.R. line to Galway; No.394 was photographed at Athenry on such a train on 30 June 1938.

There were several classes of 4-4-0 built over the years, the more modern ones to the design of R. Coey, who was locomotive superintendent from 1896 to 1911. No.336, photographed together with 0-6-0 No.129 passing Cork on a Tralee–Cobh excursion on 8 July 1934, was one of a class of ten built in 1907/8, originally unsuperheated, but later rebuilt as seen in this photograph. Five more identical engines came out in 1936. With 5′ 8½″ driving wheels, they were intended for mixed traffic duties. An express version, with 6′ 7″ wheels, may be seen in the photograph on page 10.

J.A.F. Aspinall, who succeeded MacDonnell in 1883, designed a series of somewhat similar engines, but with 6' 7" wheels for express work. Many of them acquired Belpaire fireboxes and superheaters in later years, and like the smaller engines just mentioned, the class was a long-lived one, being seen on secondary duties well into the 1950s. No.95, in unrebuilt state, is at Claremorris in June 1938. Aspinall also gravitated to England, and became C.M.E. of the Lancashire & Yorkshire until 1899. The somewhat similar 4-4-0s which he built for that railway mostly lasted into the early L.M.S. era, but again were outlived by many years by the Irish engines.

his small 4-4-0 of a type built for cross-country work with 5' 8½" wheels dated back to 1878 and was uilt by A. MacDonnell, who was locomotive superintendent at Inchicore from 1864 to 1883, when he ent to the North Eastern. On that railway he built some very similar 4-4-0s, but these all disappeared ng before the Irish engines, most of which lasted into the 1950s. No.44, at Rosslare Harbour on 28 June 938, is on a train for Wexford.

nother of the same class, No.15 of 1880, at the well known holiday resort of Killarney, 12 July 1934. lthough an intermediate station on the secondary main line from Mallow to Tralee this was actually a rminal spur, all trains having to reverse once, after running into the platform directly, to regain access to e through line, or to carry out the opposite process. In this view an up express for Cork had set back to the station before proceeding towards Mallow.

The only class of engine in Ireland which could in any way have been described as a standard design was the J15 0-6-0 of the Great Southern & Western, the first examples of which came out in 1867, when MacDonnell was locomotive superintendent. They were perpetuated at intervals by his three successors until 1903, by which time 108 of them had appeared—not a great number by British standards, but by far the most numerous of any single design to appear in Ireland. No.148 was the first, and although built in small batches not in numerical order, they eventually occupied the whole range of numbers 101-200, together with 240-243 and 253-256. The remarkable similarity to the Ramsbottom Dx engines of the L.N.W.R. which preceeded them cannot be coincidental. They were general purpose 'maids-of-all-work' mixed-traffic engines, to be seen on every conceivable kind of duty and active right to the end of the steam era, some of them still at work in the 1960s (although the first withdrawal had taken place as long ago as 1928). In later years many of them received Belpaire boilers and superheaters, and one of these, No.186, has been preserved in working order by the Railway Preservation Society of Ireland. Based on Whitehead, near Belfast, it makes extensive sorties over lines of the whole Irish railway system on enthusiasts' specials. Fortunately C.I.E. places no restrictions as to routes such as are imposed by B.R. Another, No.184, in unrebuilt condition, is also preserved. These are among the small number of Irish engines which have survived—pitifully few when compared with Great Britain. This illustration is of No.200, in unrebuilt condition and still retaining the unusual double door type of smokebox, peculiar to the Great Southern & Western, at Bray on 6 June 1932.

No.102 working the Fenit train on 13 July 1934. This eight mile branch on the south west coast of Ireland, once an independent company, opened in 1887, on which regular passenger services ceased at the end of 1934.

No.106, in rebuilt state, with a double-headed train at the eastern end of the main platform at Limerick Junction, 30 June 1938. The second locomotive is former Waterford, Limerick & Western 0-6-0 No.239. Other W.L. & W.R. engines are featured on pages 22 and 23.

J15 No.255, fitted for oil burning (during the period of the coal shortage already mentioned), at Inchicore, 16 April 1948.

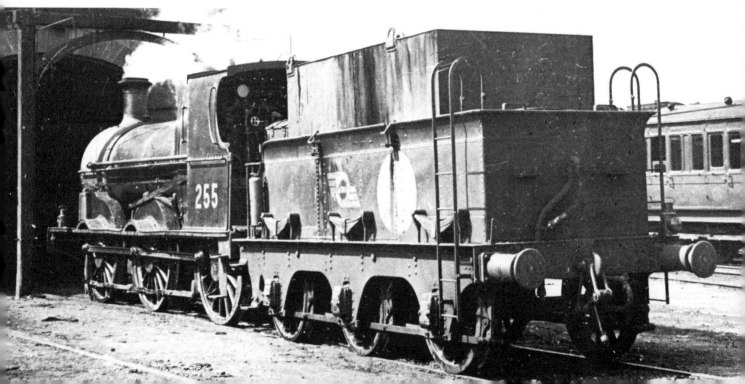

One of the more spectacular routes in Ireland was the long (39¼ mile) branch from Farranfore to Valencia Harbour, on the west coast shores of the Atlantic Ocean, which passed through magnificent mountain and coastal scenery en route. It was opened in 1893 and regrettably entirely closed in 1960. No.127 pauses at Kells, one of the intermediate passing places, on 14 April 1955.   [R. M. Casserley]

The end of the line, Valencia Harbour, on the same day. This outpost, and the buffer stop in the foreground, had the distinction of being the most westerly railhead, not only in the British Isles, but in the whole of Europe. It was closely approached in this respect by the Tralee & Dingle, on the Kerry peninsula not far to the north, but over on the other side of Dingle Bay.

Hardly representative of the 'Heyday of Steam' in Ireland, but nevertheless an interesting picture in its declining years. G. & S.W.R. Aspinall 2-4-2T No.41, transferred to the Cork Bandon section, in a picturesque setting at Upton on 13 April 1955 with the morning train to Bantry. By that date this service was normally worked by a diesel railcar, but on Wednesdays it was booked for steam haulage while the diesel was receiving its weekly maintenance. Fore-knowledge of this fact meant that the whole week's itinerary for this tour had to be worked out so that this particular trip was fitted in on the Wednesday, and advantage taken of this wonderful and probably unrepeatable opportunity. As it eventually turned out, the whole of the railway system in the south west of Cork was to be completely closed by 1961, after which even a journey in a diesel railcar, which would have been acceptable, was no longer possible. The southern Irish railway staff were usually very co-operative with an enquiry as to whether there would be an opportunity to obtain a photograph—'Sure, begorrah, don't hurry yourself; take all the *toime* you want.' [R. M. Casserley]

No.201 trundles a freight train through the streets of Cork on the connecting line between the G.S. & W.R. and the western Cork lines, 18 March 1961. There were a number of these 0-6-0Ts built around the turn of the century for shunting, to the design of H.A. Ivatt (later of Great Northern fame), who was in charge at Inchicore from 1886 to 1896.   [R.M. Casserley]

One of Aspinall's peculiar 0-4-4WTs, No.78 built in 1886, shunting at Wexford, 2 July 1938.

The Waterford
Limerick & Western
Railway, a long
straggling route throu[gh]
the western counties [of]
Ireland, from Waterfo[rd]
in the south to Sligo i[n]
the north, was taken
over by the Great
Southern & Western in
1901. The principal
main line locomotives
which the G.S. & W.R.
acquired consisted of
three handsome 4-4-0s
and five somewhat
similar 2-4-0s, all dating
from the 1890s. This
scene is of 4-4-0
No.298 at Athenry on
30 June 1938

One of the 2-4-0s,
No.290, shunting at
Waterford on 11 June
1932.

Former W.L. & W.R. 0-4-2T No.274, one of a class of five built in 1895/6, with a local train to Baltimore, near Skibbereen, on the Cork, Bandon & South Coast line, 1 July 1938.

The W.L. & W.R. had two 0-4-4Ts, built in 1895, one of which, No.295 is seen at Roscrea with the Birr branch train on 24 April 1953.

No.672 passing Grand Canal Street on 15 May 1950, one of five 0-6-2Ts of a new class built at Inchicore in 1933 to the designs of A. W. Harty, at that time locomotive superintendent of the Great Southern Railways, for the busy suburban service between Dublin and Bray.

This was one of the few areas in Ireland which had anything approaching what may be regarded as a commuter service, to use modern phraseology. The G.N.R. operated a similar pattern of trains north of the city, but the old G.S. & W.R. and M.G.W.R. to the west never had anything in the way of a suburban service. The only other Irish cities in which such busy lines could be found were around Belfast, and to a much smaller extent, Cork. Elsewhere in the sparsely populated country away from the main routes, the usual pattern of service consisted of two or three trains daily, often of a 'mixed' nature, combining a passenger coach or two with sundry goods vehicles conveying mostly livestock and farm produce. There were often lengthy stops at small wayside stations to allow time for shunting, attaching or detaching vans. It was this leisurely and peaceful atmosphere. which gave the Irish railways so much of their charm.

The only eight-coupled engines in Ireland (apart from four narrow gauge—see pages 88-90) were two heavy 4-8-0Ts, built at Inchicore by the G.S. & W.R., designed by E. A. Watson, who succeeded Maunsell in 1911. No.900 came out in 1915 and No.901 (photographed at Inchicore on 20 September 1929) in 1924. They had short lives by Irish standards, No.900 being withdrawn in 1928 and the second one three years later.

A solitary 2-6-2T, No.850, which came out from Inchicore in 1928, designed by J. R. Bazin, was built for working the Dun Laoghaire boat trains, but does not seem to have been very popular on this service. It was scrapped in 1955. Photographed at Bray on 6 June 1932.

Another post-amalgamation G.S.R. class was the J15A, designed by W. H. Morton, consisting of five engines, Nos.700-704, built at Inchicore in 1929; No.704 at Amiens Street Dublin, 20 July 1934.

They were intended to be a modernised version of the J15s, but neither these nor their successors, Nos.710-719, of Class J15B, which appeared in 1934-5, were found to be in any way superior to the original well-tried J15s; none of them, in spite of their comparative newness, lasted quite as long as the final survivors of those remarkable engines.

The Dublin & South Eastern Railway, the nucleus of which was the Dublin & Kingstown, the first railway in Ireland, provided a little over forty engines which came into G.S.R. stock at the 1925 amalgamation, which became Nos. 422-462 under the new regime. This included five 4-4-0s, chiefly used on the main line between Dublin, Wexford and Rosslare; No.453 at Bray on 17 September 1929.

All engines had carried names, except the last four to be built, but these were latterly removed. No.453 had formerly been No.58 *Rathdrum*. The livery was black, lined out with red and orange.

The newest engines were a couple of 2-6-0s, Nos.461 and 462, which came out in 1922 as D.S.E.R. Nos.15 and 16, for main line goods work. No.462 leaving Wexford on 2 July 1938; the other of the pair has been preserved.

Over half of the D.S.E.R. locomotive stock consisted of tank engines for the busy Bray suburban service, 2-4-0Ts, 2-4-2Ts, and 4-4-2Ts. One of these, 2-4-2T No.436 (late D.S.E.R.27, formerly *St. Aiden*) was photographed at Harcourt Street on 16 May 1950. Harcourt Street was a second terminus in Dublin for D.S.E.R. trains, taking an inland route from Bray, secondary to the main line which followed the coast line to Westland Row and Amiens Street station. The whole branch was closed in 1959.

The Midland Great Western was the third largest railway in Ireland, exceeded in importance only by the Great Northern and the Great Southern & Western. The 129 locomotives taken over at the 1925 amalgamation by the G.S.R. were re-numbered 530-668 consecutively in one block, grouped according to class. The great majority were tender engines, 2-4-0s, 4-4-0s and 0-6-0s, the last two of several varieties. Some of the 4-4-0s were rebuilds of earlier 2-4-0s. No.546 late M.G.W.R. No.129 *Celtic*, photographed at the old Broadstone terminus in Dublin, now closed, on 7 June 1932, was about to leave with the 7.20 a.m. Galway mail train. The Midland Great Western had pursued a policy of naming the whole of its locomotive stock up to 1921, when the practice was abandoned; these were all removed by the newly created Great Southern, and the green livery gave way to the grey/black of the G.S.R.

The express 4-4-0s had 6′ 3″ driving wheels, but there was also a series of smaller engines with 5′ 8″ wheels, mainly for the long western branches. These were usually known as the *Achill bogies* (somewhat in the manner of the *Skye bogies* of the Highland Railway). No.534, late No.5 *Britannia*, rebuilt with superheater and Belpaire firebox, is entering Newport with an Achill-Dublin train 18 July 1934. This scenic route on the west coast of Ireland, together with the somewhat similar Clifden branch, were early casualties, having been completely closed as early as 1937 and 1935 respectively.

No.651 again, now rebuilt with Belpaire firebox and superheater—a rare distinction for old engines of this type, and possibly unique—at Claremorris on 29 June 1938 with a train for Athlone.

he M.G.W.R. had a stud of nineteen 2-4-0s at the amalgamation, all built during the 1890s and which became G.S.R. os.650-668. All remained in service until the 1950s, and a few even into the early 1960s, the last of their kind in the ritish Isles. It was a great pity that one of them was not preserved and indeed that no M.G.W.R. engine now survives. o.651, late No.16 *Rob Roy,* largely in original condition with its distinctive flared cab, much used on earlier M.G. .R. engines and better exemplified in the illustration on page 36, at Westport on 17 July 1934, about to depart for ublin.

2-4-0 No.655 (formerly No.29 *Clonsilla*) with a train from Westport entering Manulla Junction, 20 April 1955 bound for Mullingar, about to pick up the single line tablet. These engines were still to be seen at this period on main line trains carrying express headlights, and on one occasion we did on this visit have a run on the evening mail train for Sligo behind one of these engines, the stock of which included a 12 wheeled coach with clerestory roof and ornate fittings together with gas lighting—a real vintage throw-back to the Edwardian era.

No.656 (late M.G.W. No.30 *Active*) with the branch train at Loughrea, 21 April 1955. The contrast in stock will be noted, an old six wheeled brake together with a modern side-corridor bogie coach. No prizes for guessing which of the vehicles we elected to travel in, notwithstanding exhortations from the guard: 'You'll be much more comfortable in the bogie Sorr!' This particular branch was unique in that it still remained open throughout the 1960s and did not finally lose its passenger service until November 1975. By that time it was the last purely rural branch of its kind still run as a locomotive-hauled mixed train (albeit of course latterly with a diesel engine) and not the inevitable railcar—not only in Ireland, but the whole of the British Isles. While still steam-worked, it was also the last haunt of the M.G.W.R. 2-4-0s.

In 1929 there were still a fe[w]
M.G.W.R. engines which ha[d]
not yet received their new
numbers and been de-name[d.]
One such was 0-6-0 No.74 *L*[a]
(to become G.S.R. No.576)
Broadstone, 17 September
1929. The unique type of
flared cab carried by many
M.G.W.R. engines was
gradually replaced by a mor[e]
orthodox type.

The 0-6-0 was the most
numerous type employed on
the M.G.W.R; there were 78
of them of several classes,
which became G.S.R.
Nos.563-613 and 619-649
(Nos.623-645, built in 1921-4
were never named). One of
the earlier ones was No.582
(formerly No.73 *Comet*), here
rebuilt with Belpaire firebox
and superheater, entering
Moycullen with a Clifden-
Galway train, 16 July 1934.
This long branch was one of
the first to be closed, in 1935.

The only later tank engines on the M.G.W.R. were of the 0-6-0T type, of two classes, which became G.S.R. 551-562 and 614-618. The smaller of these two varieties, although not the oldest, were sometimes used on the shorter branch lines, but the more general practice was to employ tender engines on such duties. Three of these 0-6-0Ts were sent to the Waterford & Tramore after the demise of that Railway's own ancient locomotives (see pages 40/41) to work the line pending the introduction of diesel railcars until its final closure in 1960. No.560 (formerly M.G.W.R. No.115 *Achill*) at Waterford **Manor Street** on 12 April 1955, heads some of the later coaching stock which had replaced earlier vehicles, and which were in fact a conversion from Clayton steam railcars. These had been built in 1928 for branch line work, but had not proved too successful.

The Cork, Bandon & South Coast Railway, together with the smaller Cork & Macroom, formed the principal network serving the south west coast of Ireland which now no longer possesses any rail system. The locomotive stock consisted entirely of tank engines, several of them being 4-6-0Ts, an unusual type rarely found elsewhere in the British Isles. One of these, No.465, is seen outside Drimoleague shed on 1 July 1938.

At the C.B. & S.C.R. yard at Cork, headquarters of the line, most of the engines were kept in the open, there never being any covered accommodation. The two 4-4-2Ts are C.B. & S.C.R. No.479 and G.S. & W.R. No.31, photographed on 15 September 1929.

No.464, one of the last survivors, in a pictorial setting on Innishannon viaduct, near Bandon, on a final rail-tour of the line on 17 March 1961.

[R.M. Casserley]

The Waterford & Tramore was a 7¼ mile line entirely isolated from any other rail connection, opened in 1853 and running from the south bank of the river at Waterford to the seaside resort of Tramore. There was no intermediate station. When it was absorbed into the G.S.R. in 1925, the locomotive stock consisted of two ancient 2-2-2WTs built by Fairbairn in 1855, a 0-4-2WT dating back to 1862, and a more modern 0-4-2T of 1908. These were allocated Nos.483-486 in the G.S.R. list. One of the single wheelers was scrapped in 1928, leaving the survivor as the star performer and attraction to enthusiasts. On 11 June 1932 No.483 (late W. & T. No.1) was still actively engaged, as seen in this photograph taken near Tramore. This gallant little 80 year old remained at work until August 1935 when it was unfortunately derailed and rolled down an embankment. Regrettably it was cut up on the spot, otherwise it might have continued in service long enough to become a very worth-while candidate for preservation. It was almost the last single wheeler in Great Britain and Ireland to remain in active service.

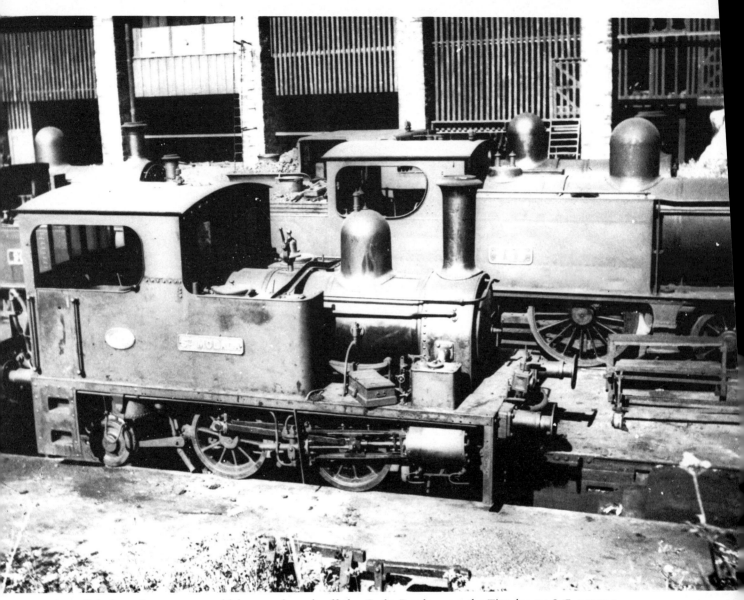

A small independent concern which was a branch off the Cork, Bandon was the Timoleague & Courtmac-sherry, a mainly roadside line worked by two very dissimilar engines. This is 0-4-2T *St. Molaga,* at the C.B. & S.C.R. yard on 7 July 1934; the other engine was *Argadeen,* a 2-6-0T with inside cylinders.

0-6-4T No.92, built in 1880, and used as an inspectors' saloon, was latterly used for conveying st. personnel between Inchicore works and Kingsbridge station; photographed at Inchicore, September 19

gh the G.S. & W.R. had
ed the naming of engines
ny years, it did have a few
mental ones which bore
only, the principle
ently being that an engine
have either a name or a
er, but not both! This
s little specimen, *Sprite*
in 1873), which seems
nearly all wheels but very
boiler, once toured the
m with a four-wheel saloon
n as a pay carriage, for
buting wages to outlying
cts. There was also a sister
e *Fairy*. When photographed
chicore in September 1929
e was acting as a stationary
er for supplying steam. Others
his delightful miscellaneous
rtment included *Sambo, Jumbo*
Erin.

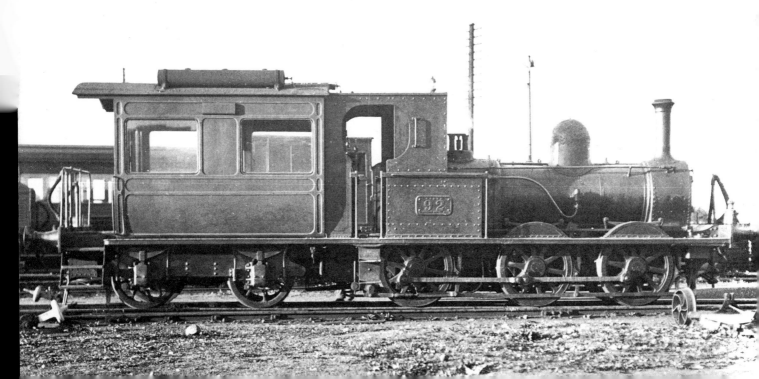

Although the normal gauge in Ireland was 5′ 3″ there was also a considerable mileage built to a secondary standard of 3′ 0″ for light railways in rural areas, and several of these which lay wholly within the newly constituted Irish Free State were inevitably absorbed into the G.S.R. in 1925. Two of them, the Cork & Muskerry Light Railway and the Cork, Blackrock & Passage, hardly came into the category of rural branch lines, in that both of them had terminals well within the boundaries of the city. This was especially the case with the C.B. & P.R. which had its own reserved track and ranked more as a suburban railway. The C. & M.L.R. was actually a roadside tramway, serving the western parts of Cork and running out to the famous Blarney Castle, and a branch to Coachford. This view shows a train leaving the Cork terminus on 15 September 1929, with 0-4-4T No.5K, one of a pair built in 1892/3.

Another view on the outskirts of Cork on 10 June 1932, with engine No.2K. Narrow gauge engines were not renumbered by the G.S.R. but kept their own numbers with a distinguishing suffix, K being the letter applied to the Muskerry. The line through the streets of Western Road was parallel to an adjacent track on which ran cars of the Cork City Tramways. Although these had ceased running the previous September, in 1931, the gantry formerly carrying the overhead wiring is still in position. The C. & M.R. itself ceased operations at the end of 1934, but it had outlasted its rivals by three years. Unfortunately neither was really suited to withstand the impact of road competition.

As already stated, the Cork, Blackrock & Passage was really an urban line originally of 5′ 3″ gauge and dating back to 1850, but converted to 3′ 0″ around the turn of the century. Along its sixteen miles by the western shores of Cork Harbour there were numerous curves, but nevertheless speeds of 50 m.p.h. were often attained—high for a narrow gauge. The engines were four 2-4-2Ts, built in 1899, Nos.4-7, of somewhat clumsy appearance, but quite stable in spite of their top-heavy aspect. This view shows Nos.6P, 5P and 7P in the shed yard at Cork, Albert Road, 10 June 1932.

On the closure of the C.B. & P.R. in 1932 the four engines were transferred to another 3′ 0″ system, the Cavan & Leitrim, and to avoid confusion with that company's existing locomotives they were renumbered from 4P-7P (the Passage designation) to 10L-13L. There they had several further years of useful life, Nos.10L and 12L even until the demise of the Cavan & Leitrim in 1959, one of the last of the narrow gauge lines to succumb. No.13L was photographed at Ballyconnell with a mixed train on 17 May 1950.

The Cavan & Leitrim Railway, referred to on the previous page, was purely a rural line in the northern part of the central plain of Ireland, with a route mileage of 52 miles. The locomotive stock consisted of eight 4-4-0Ts, Nos.1-8, and one 0-6-4T, No.9. No.1 *Isabel*, later denamed and known as No.1L, stands at Dromod, the southern extremity, where the line made contact with the M.G.W.R. main route to Sligo; 7 June 1932.

The headquarters and general workshops of the line were at Ballinamore, where most of the engines were to be found, and which was a junction for Arigna, where was mined one of the few small deposits of coal to be found in Ireland. The 'main line' continued north to Belturbet, also served by a branch of the Great Northern. On 15 April 1948, No.2L is about to leave for Ballinamore from the narrow gauge platform, the broad lines of the G.N.R. lying on the right. This engine, *Kathleen,* is now in Belfast Museum, and No.3 *Lady Edith* is preserved in the U.S.A. The final train ran on 31 March 1959, almost the last of the C.I.E. narrow gauge lines, only beaten by the West Clare, which survived until 1961.

In the south west corner of Ireland was the Schull & Skibbereen, which left the main line of the Cork, Bandon & South Coast and ran for fifteen miles, largely along the roadside, and around the shores of Roaring Water Bay to the small coastal village of Schull. This mixed train is about to depart from Skibbereen on 16 September 1929 with 4-4-0T No.1 *Gabriel*. This locomotive was later known as No.1S, but unlike most G.S.R. engines, retained its name until scrapped in 1936, as did No.3 *Kent*. To replace No.1, another engine was transferred to the line in 1936 from the Cork & Muskerry; this was No.6, similar to the one illustrated on page 44, and renumbered 6S, but does not seem to have been used to any extent.

Another 4-4-0T, No.4S, formerly No.4 *Erin,* pauses at a roadside halt at Kilcoe on 1 July 1938. Services ceased in July 1947, but the line was not officially closed until 1952.

Two narrow gauge lines which ran to the west coast also survived until the 1950s, as did the Cavan & Leitrim. The West & South Clare, actually two separate systems with end-on connection at Miltown Malbay, but in practice worked as one, ran from the Waterford, Limerick & Western at Ennis to Moyasta Junction, from which diverged two branches—to Kilrush, on the mouth of the Shannon, and to Kilkee, on the shores of Galway Bay. The journey to Kilkee, the main terminus, 48 miles from Ennis, took about three hours. The locomotives which came into the stock of the G.S.R. in 1925 consisted of two 0-6-2Ts, four 2-6-2Ts, and five 4-6-0Ts. They had all previously carried names which were removed on amalgamation, when they became known as 1C-11C. 0-6-2T No.6C on a train leaving Ennis, 30 June 1938. This was the last of the G.S.R. narrow gauge lines remaining open until 1961. It was the only one to go over to diesel traction, at first with railcars and later with locomotives, of which three were built in 1955, the only narrow gauge ones on C.I.E.

The Tralee & Dingle was another picturesque route, 37½ miles long, which has already been mentioned on page 19 as being almost, but not quite, the most westerly railhead in Europe. Passenger services ceased in April 1939, but continued for freight until 1947. Thereafter there were one or two cattle trains once a month on Dingle Fair Day, and these continued until final closure in June 1953. In the final years these specials became famous in the railway enthusiasts' world, and visitors came from far and wide, especially from England, to take a last opportunity of travelling over one of Ireland's most spectacular railways, permits to travel being readily granted by C.I.E. Such views, together with photographs of the T. & D. in its earlier days, appear in abundance in a companion volume by D. G. Rowlands devoted entirely to this railway. This view however, shows one of the last pictures taken of a Tralee & Dingle engine at work. Two of the 2-6-0Ts, Nos.3T and 4T, were transferred to the Cavan & Leitrim line, where they remained in service until that line's closure in 1959 and No.3 is seen here with the Arigna branch train on 17 March of that year.

[R. M. Casserley]

Ireland's second largest railway, the Great Northern, could be regarded as the most enterprising and progressive in the whole country, more in line with those on this side of the Irish Sea, and in some ways not unlike its English namesake, although it had no direct affiliation with the G.N.R. over here. This is not to disparage the main line railways in the south, all very efficiently run, but taking into account the more leisurely tempo of the Republic as a whole, more particularly in the rural areas. In the north, the N.C.C. in particular, part of the L.M.S. system at the grouping, inherited the lively go-ahead traditions of its earlier owners, the Midland. One must also not forget the smartly operated County Down. The introduction of the 'Enterprise Express' in 1932 was a great step forward in fast rail travel in Ireland, the 112½ miles between Belfast and Dublin being covered in 125 minutes. It incorporated Ireland's first 60 m.p.h. booking, the 54.3 miles between Dublin and Dundalk being scheduled to be covered in 54 minutes. It must be remembered that the overall time between the two cities included stops of several minutes at Goraghwood or Dundalk, according to direction, for customs examination, and was equivalent to what would otherwise have been a booking of about 115 minutes. For the new service five splendid 4-4-0 three-cylinder compounds were built by Beyer Peacock & Co., who supplied a large proportion of the company's engines over the years. This is No.84 at Amiens Street on the first day of operation, 4 June 1932, in readiness for the inaugural run. G.N.R. engines at one time nearly all carried names, but these had been removed between 1915 and 1920. The new locomotives revived this practice to some extent, appearing as No.83 *Eagle*, No.84 *Falcon*, No.85 *Merlin*, No.86 *Peregrine* and No.87 *Kestrel*.

They were in later years fitted with Belpaire boilers and No.86 is seen here on a southbound express passing Dundalk Square Crossing (where the G.N.R. crossed the Dundalk, Newry & Greenore Railway; see page 66). No.85 is seen on the works siding to the left, outshopped after overhaul, and painted in the new blue livery which had been adopted for the principal express types; 15 May 1950.

Overleaf:

In 1947 it was found possible to eliminate the Goraghwood and Dundalk stops, arrangements having been made to carry out the customs examinations at sealed-off platforms at the two terminals. A second train was introduced in May 1948, and five new engines, again 4-4-0s, very similar to the compounds, but this time with three cylinder simple propulsion, appeared. These were Nos.206 *Liffey*, 207 *Boyne*, 208 *Lagan*, 209 *Foyle* and 210 *Erne*, again from the works of Beyer Peacock, of Manchester. They were the last main line 4-4-0s to be built, certainly in the British Isles and possibly anywhere in the world. The reason that the G.N.R. never had a 4-6-0 was dictated by the length of the traversers in Dundalk locomotive works, which could not accommodate a ten-wheeled engine. However, the service ran extremely well with 4-4-0s to the end of steam working, and the two series could in many ways be compared with the very similar L.M.S. Compounds and the Southern 'Schools', which could probably be regarded as the ultimate developments of the 4-4-0 type. It has already been recounted (page 11) that between 1950 and 1953 the 'Enterprise' ran through to Cork in conjunction with C.I.E., the 278 miles representing the longest through service ever to operate in Ireland. The 'Enterprise' express may rightly be regarded as representing the Heyday of Steam in Ireland. No.208 is on the southbound train near Dundalk, 15 May 1950.

Another of the 'Rivers', No.209 *Foyle* leaving Amiens Street on the northbound 'Enterprise', 16 April 1955.

Before the arrival of the 'Birds' and the 'Rivers', the principal express locomotive on the G.N.R. had been inside-cylinder 4-4-0s of several varieties, the largest of which were Nos.190-192, dating back to 1915. They were rebuilt in 1938 and named *Lugnaquilla*, *Croagh Patrick*, and *Slievenamon*, and also received the newly-introduced striking blue livery with red underframes; No.192 at Dundalk 14 April 1948.

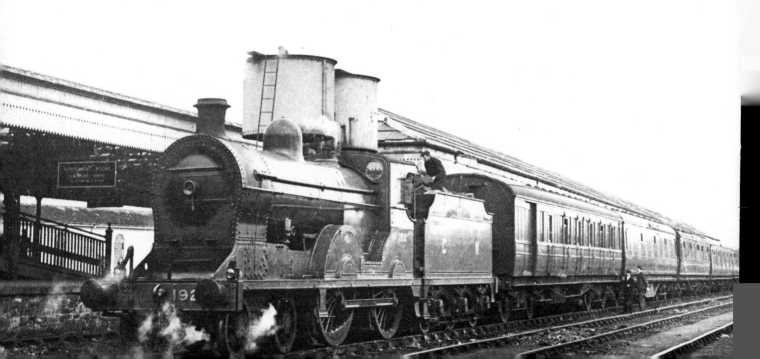

Small-boilered 4-4-0 No.129 piloting No.135 with a Belfast to Londonderry express at Dungannon, 13 April 1948.

One illustration to show that steam is not quite extinct in the Emerald Isle, if only on a preservation basis—No.171 *Slieve Gullion* was acquired by the Railway Preservation Society of Ireland and is used for extensive tours of the country, including the Republic, as C.I.E. have fortunately proved very co-operative in this respect. This fine 4-4-0 is here at Wellington Bridge, between Rosslare and Waterford, a long way from its native system, on 16 September 1973.

Almost concurrently with the five large 4-4-0s built in 1948, the G.N.R. rather surprisingly perpetuated an intermediate cross-country type of 4-4-0 which had first appeared in 1915 by obtaining five more in 1947, again from Beyer Peacock. This was a curious propagation at so late a date of what was almost an Edwardian design. The only noticeable modification was in the tender, which was of more modern type. These were Nos.201 *Meath*, 202 *Louth*, 203 *Armagh*, 204 *Antrim* and 205 *Down*. Classified as express types for publicity purposes, they received the new blue livery. No.204 is piloting compound No.83 on a northbound express leaving Dundalk on 14 April 1948.

At the same time, the five original engines were updated by the application of blue livery and bestowal of names, Nos.196 *Lough Gill,* 197 *Lough Neagh,* 198 *Lough Swilly,* 199 *Lough Derg* and 200 *Lough Melvin.* No.197 at Clones, 18 April 1955.

A close-up of the new style of nameplate adopted in later years. Before 1920 these had been substantial oblong plates usually attached to the boiler, as on the M.G.W.R. This illustration of No.201, taken in April 1948, also shows the G.N.R. coat of arms, and Beyer Peacock works plate (7244 of 1947) This was destined to be among the last of a long line of steam locomotives, many for overseas, built over a period of about 100 years before turning over to the production of diesels, with which the company was unfortunately nothing like so successful; regrettably the firm closed in 1966.

Nos.88 and 89 were originally built in 1889 (also by Beyer Peacock) as 4-2-2 single wheelers, the only ones of the type ever to run in Ireland. Named *Victoria* and *Albert* they were reconstructed in 1904 at Dundalk as 4-4-0s. This is No.89 at Newry, 4 June 1932.

The new 4-4-0 compounds of 1932 indirectly replaced the last remaining engines of the 2-4-0 type, whose numbers they took. There were four of them, dating back to 1880/1, Nos.84/87. Selected to illustrate the class is No.86, engaged in local shunting at Newry, 4 June 1932.

No.104, one of a class of small 4-4-0s with 5′ 6″ wheels for cross-country and branch line work, approaching Bundoran Junction, in September 1929, with the 'Bundoran Express', which served the watering place of that name on the shores of Donegal Bay. Along with the rest of the G.N.R. system in North West Ireland, this 35½ mile branch off the main line to Londonderry was ruthlessly closed by the Northern Ireland government under its anti-rail policy during the late 1950s, a sad end to the larger part of what was once a well-run and prosperous railway system.

The 0-6-0 naturally found an integral place in the locomotive stock, as on the other railways being grouped roughly into categories A to D according to engine power. No.141 of Class A, seen at Clones on 18 April 1955, might well at first glance be mistaken for an engine of the English G.N.R, with which the Irish line in fact had no connection.

0-6-0 No.100, of Class B, entering the Belfast Central Terminus (now closed) in June 1937, with a suburban train from Portadown. Space does not allow illustrations of the similar but larger boilered C and D classes.

Amiens Street shed at Dublin on 6 June 1932, with three of the 4-4-2Ts used for suburban services out of the city to Howth and northwards towards Drogheda. The G.N.R. had a fleet of 27 of these useful engines for suburban work, built between 1913 and 1929.

Another 4-4-2T, No.63, at Antrim on 26 June 1937, with a local train for Belfast.

The Dundalk, Newry & Greenore Railway was a small concern, entirely English-owned throughout its existence, being an offshoot of the L.N.W.R., and in turn of its successors, the L.M.S. and British Railways. Situated partly in Northern Ireland and partly in the Free State, it did not come within the orbit of the Great Southern at the 1925 amalgamation. In its last years it was operated by the Great Northern, and was completely closed in 1951. The six engines, all 0-6-0STs, were of L.N.W.R. design, and were in fact built at Crewe between 1873 and 1898. No.4 *Newry,* seen passing over the Great Northern main line at Dundalk, is bound for Newry and Greenore on 15 May 1950. A view of a G.N.R. train at this location appears on page 58.

The Dublin & Blessington was a roadside tramway of a kind which survived in Ireland well into the inter-war period. It was however of standard gauge instead of the narrow 3' 0" and continued to use double-decker tramcar vehicles until the final closure in 1932. Double-ended 2-4-2T No.10 heads along the main High Street at Blessington, 5 June 1932.

A view from the upper deck of one of the tram coaches, taken on the same date, gives some idea of what a journey could be like, ideal for the enthusiast who does not mind a few smuts and particularly enjoys a whiff of a mixture of smoke and steam—hard to find nowadays.

e Belfast & Northern Counties was absorbed by the Midland Railway of England in 1903 it was the fourth ystem in Ireland, with a route mileage of 265, of which 64 was of the 3′ 0″ narrow gauge. It became part of the t the 1923 grouping, and in its later years was a sheer joy to lovers of the old M.R. Many of the engines showed Midland ancestry and some were in fact built at Derby. All of them, passenger and goods, were painted in the crimson lake and moreover kept in spick and span condition. The locomotive superintendent from 1876 to as Bowman Malcolm, his reign of forty six years in this position possibly constituting a record. All of the he built between 1890 and 1908 were two-cylinder Worsdell von Borries compounds, mostly 2-4-0s and 4-4-0s. *Parkmount,* photographed in Belfast works on 5 August 1930, was one of a pair of seven footers, the largest driving wheels ever used in Ireland. This example was scrapped in 1944 without being rebuilt, but most of the unds were latterly converted to simple propulsion.

Sister engine No.50 *Jubilee,* rebuilt as a two-cylinder simple, approaching Larne Harbour with a boat express on 9 April 1930. Both of these engines had been built by Beyer Peacock in 1895 as 2-4-0s, the bogie being provided at a later date. No.50 was scrapped in 1946.

Compound 2-4-0 No.57 *Galgorm Castle* leaving Cookstown Junction on 20 June 1938 with a train for Cookstown.

No.23 a 2-4-0 with ordinary two cylinder simple propulsion, built in 1885, at Coleraine shed 26 June 1937. This engine lasted until 1942.

A close-up of the cylinder arrangement of *Galgorm Castle,* showing the small high pressure cylinder on the left (as viewed from the camera) and the large low pressure one on the right. A striking feature of these unusual engines, when seen—or rather heard—at work was the slow beat of the exhaust, only two beats per revolution of the driving wheels instead of the usual four (or six on some three-cylinder engines, and even eight with the S.R. 'Lord Nelsons'). They were in consequence somewhat slow in acceleration.

This outside-framed
2-4-0 (No.41) was a
veteran of 1872, in which
year it was turned out
from the works of
Messrs Sharp Stewart &
Co. of Glasgow. Seen
shunting at London-
derry on 6 August 1930,
resplendent in Midland
red and with polished
brasswork over the
splasher, it made a
splendid sight. The
tender, it will be noted,
was lettered, L.M.S.-
N.C.C. (Northern
Counties Committee).
This engine was scrapped
in 1933.

In 1933 the 2-6-0 type was introduced for main line express work, the first four of which were built at Derby, Nos. 90-93. The last of these, No.93 *The Foyle*, passes Coleraine at speed on 26 July 1937 with a Londonderry express. Eleven more, Nos.94-104, were assembled at intervals in the railway's own workshops at Belfast, most of the parts being supplied by Derby, between 1934 and 1942.

The last steam engines to be built for the N.C.C. were these 2-6-4Ts, based very largely on the Fowler type introduced by the L.M.S. in 1927, but with 6' 0" driving wheels instead of the 5' 9" of the parent company. All eighteen were built at Derby, Nos.1-10 in 1946/7, and Nos.50-57 in 1949/50. No.52, photographed at Londonderry on 20 May 1950, is about to depart with an express for Belfast. A few of these engines survived as late as 1970, although only on ballast work, such few remaining passenger services as still remained under the ruthless hands of the Ulster Transport Authority having been given over entirely to diesel railcars, with the exception of the 'Enterprise Express', for which three new diesel locomotives were obtained. These 2-6-4Ts were the last steam engines on regular work in Ireland, and No.4, which has been secured by the Irish Railway Preservation Society, sometimes runs specially chartered trains to Portrush during the summer months, and also participating in rail tours over the whole country, including the lines of the Irish Republic.

ndard 0-6-0T L.M.S. 'Jinties' were sent over in 1944 after having been regauged to 5′ 3″. Originally
Nos.7456 and 7553, they became N.C.C. Nos.18 and 19. The former is here at Belfast on 17
948. Tank engines had been very rare on the N.C.C. broad gauge lines and it was not until the
ance of the 2-6-4Ts that they appeared in any numbers.

The 4-4-0s had been of several classes, the history of which is somewhat complex owing to reconstruction from two
cylinder compounds to simples, some of them being rebuilds of 2-4-0s, and variously renumbered. No.77, however
(seen entering Londonderry on 19 May 1950) was of later construction, having been built by the North British Loco
Co. in 1924. Its strong Midland characteristics are very evident. A naming policy was introduced in 1930 and most of
the 4-4-0s received names in due course as did the 2-6-0s. These later 4-4-0s were known as 'Castles', but somehow
No.77, which would have been *Balleygalley Castle,* remained un-named. No.74 *Dunluce Castle,* is preserved in Belfast
Museum.

old 0-6-0, No.7, built in 1873, with a local train at Ballymena on 9 August 1930.

The N.C.C. acquired three 3′ 0″ narrow gauge systems, one of which was the Ballycastle; 0-6-0T No.106 is seen there at Ballycastle itself on 20 August 1930. This engine, one of three, had originally been built for the Ballymena & Larne Railway.

On the other hand, 4-4-2T No. 113, which, together with No. 114, was originally a Ballycastle engine, had been transferred to the Ballymena & Larne Railway. On 22 June 1937 it was working a ballast train near Larne Harbour, where the broad and narrow gauge lines ran alongside each other.

Odd man out of the 3' 0" engines was this 2-6-0ST No.109, with the Doagh branch train at Ballyboley in August 1930.

The principal engines in use on the N.C.C. narrow gauge in later years were the 2-4-2T Worsdell von Borries compounds. No.42 was built at Derby as late as 1920, many years after the appearance of the last broad gauge two-cylinder compounds. This view of her at Belfast on 14 April 1948 shows one of the transporter wagons needed to convey these engines to and from their respective branches for a works overhaul.

The Belfast & County Down was a lively railway serving most of the area to the south of Belfast, with a virtual mono-poly in the eastern part of County Down, and a total route mileage of 80 miles. Although its real main line extended as far south as Newcastle, with various branches, the most important section was the 12 miles from Belfast to Bangor, a seaside resort with a busy daily commuter and seasonal holiday traffic. This is the only part of the system which survived the ravages of the Ulster Transport Authority. This view, taken on 20 June 1938, shows a train leaving the Queens Quay terminus in Belfast (now transferred to the new Belfast Central station, served also by trains of the former G.N.R. and N.C.C.). The engine is 4-4-2T No.21, built by Beyer Peacock in 1921. Nearly all County Down engines came from the works of this firm, as had a large proportion of the G.N.R.

The same engine, now renumbered Ulster Transport Authority No.221, with a Bangor train near Carnalea on 14 May 1950. B.C.D.R. engines had 200 added to their numbers to avoid confusion with the N.C.C. There were still a number of six-wheeled vehicles in use to the end of steam working in 1954, by which time diesel multiple units had taken over. For many years the locomotive stock had been maintained at a total of thirty engines of no less than eleven different classes, the most numerous being twelve of these 4-4-2Ts, together with another three with larger boilers. One of these latter, No.9, had been built as recently as 1945 and was destined to have a working life of only eleven years. One of the smaller ones, No.30, can be seen in Belfast Museum.

...gest B.C.D.R. engines were four 4-6-4Ts, built by Beyer Peacock & Co. in 1920. Rather surprisingly, for such a ... design, they were unsuperheated: No.24 at Belfast, 5 August 1930. The B.C.D.R. livery was a rich dark green, ... to the old Great Central, lined out red and white.

The rest of the miscellaneous B.C.D.R. stock comprised four 2-4-2Ts, one 0-6-4T, and five tender engines—one 2-4-0 and four 0-6-0s of three distinct classes. The smallest of these was No.26, built by Beyer Peacock in 1892, and seen here with a local train at Holywood on 13 April 1948. The 2nd class on the coaches will be noted; all three classes were maintained until the end of locomotive hauled trains.   [R.M. Casserley]

...he oldest remaining B.C.D.R. engine in the between-the-wars period was 0-4-2T No.9, built in 1887.
...lthough little used in later years, it was not scrapped until 1949, by which time it had become No.28;
...otographed at Belfast, 5 August 1930.

The Sligo, Leitrim & Northern Counties was a lengthy standard gauge 5′ 3″ railway, running from Enniskillen in County Fermanagh, where it made connection with the G.N.R. main line to Londonderry, through Leitrim, and terminating at Sligo. This was some 48 miles in all, of which the last 5 miles or so were over the lines of the Great Southern. There were no branches, the traffic being mainly agricultural and conveyance of livestock. As the line straddled the border between the Free State and Northern Ireland, it retained independence until enforced closure came about in 1957, necessitated by the severance of its eastern link with the outside world when the Northern Ireland government decreed that all the G.N.R. lines in the north west of the country were to be abandoned in favour of road transport. In later years the engines were nearly all 0-6-4Ts; the earliest ones, built by Beyer Peacock between 1882 and 1899, were of somewhat singular and archaic appearance, as depicted in this photograph of *Hazlewood*, taken on 19 September 1929 at Manorhamilton. This was the centre of the system, and where the workshops and headquarters were situated. S.L. & N.C.R. engines were never numbered, being known by their names only. These 0-6-4Ts were respectively *Fermanagh, Leitrim, Lurganboy, Lissadell* and *Hazlewood*.

0-6-4T *Lissadell* near Manorhamilton on 29 June 1938 with a train bound for Enniskillen. Below; the same train, earlier in its journey at Ballysodare, where the S.L. & N.C.R. had running powers over the G.S.R. main line from Sligo as far as Collooney Junction.

Three further 0-6-4Ts of a more modern design appeared in 1904, 1905 and 1917, named *Sir Henry, Enniskillen,* and *Lough Gill.* The last mentioned heads a typical freight train at Manorhamilton on 29 June 1938.

There were also two 0-6-0s purchased from the G.N.R. (others worked on the line at various times) known as *Glencar* and *Sligo.* The latter is seen approaching Sligo on 29 June 1938.

In spite of the precarious outlook on the future fortunes of the railway, the company optimistically ordered two further 0-6-4Ts from Beyer Peacock, which were built in 1949 and named *Lough Melvin* and *Lough Erne*. Unfortunately they were unable to pay for them owing to the non-receipt as anticipated of a loan of £22,000 in the form of 'grant aid' from the Northern Ireland government; this failed to materialise, and it was not until a hire purchase agreement had been concluded with Messrs Beyer Peacock & Co. in 1951 that they were delivered. They were notable in being the last new conventional steam locomotives built for any railway in the whole of Ireland. When the line closed in 1957 they were sold by the makers, as owners, to the Ulster Transport Authority, and worked for a few more years at Belfast. On withdrawal in 1966, *Lough Melvin* was purchased privately for preservation and is now at the Whitehead premises of the Irish Railway Preservation Society. This illustration is of *Lough Erne* near Florencourt on 18 May 1955.

Overleaf:

The Londonderry & Lough Swilly Railway, together with the associated Letterkenny & Burtonport Extension, was worked as one system by the L. & L.S.R. With a total mileage of 99 miles, it was one of the most extensive of the 3' 0" gauge lines, exceeded only by the neighbouring County Donegal. Its Londonderry terminus and headquarters was actually in Northern Ireland, but most of the system lay within the Free State in Donegal. The Burtonport Extension ran through some of the wildest and most mountainous parts of the country, terminating at the small fishing port of Burtonport. The fifty mile journey from Letterkenny took about three hours—a fascinating journey which still lingers as one's most happy memories of a lifetime of exploration of the railways of the British Isles. Here, the return morning train from Burtonport (two trains ran each way daily) stops to take water at Creeslough, one of the lonely intermediate stations, on 24 June 1937, in charge of one of two 4-8-0 tender engines (Nos.11 and 12) built in 1905 by Hudswell Clarke & Co. for working the line. There were also two massive 4-8-4Ts, but these spent most of their time on other parts of the L. & L.S.R. nearer to Londonderry. Apart from the two G.S.R. 4-8-0Ts illustrated on page 26, these were the only eight-coupled engines ever to run in Ireland. They were also the only examples of their respective wheel arrangements, 4-8-0 and 4-8-4T, in the British Isles.

4-8-4Ts already referred to were Nos.5 and 6, also from Hudswell Clarke, and built in 1912. No.5 is seen here …nderry, Pennyburn, on 6 August 1930.

4-6-0T No.2 is here working an excursion to Buncrana on 24 June 1937, leaving Londonderry and having just passed over a road level crossing and entering Pennyburn, where the headquarters and workshops of the line were situated. All remaining rail services on the L. & L.S.R. finally ceased in 1953. Oddly enough, the Londonderry & Lough Swilly Railway Company still exists as such, although in name only, as for many years it has continued to operate only road services.

…s.1 to 4 were 4-6-0Ts, built by Andrew Barclay of Kilmarnock in 1902 for the opening of the Burtonport Extension …d in fact lettered L. & B.E.R. on the tank sides, as were some of the remaining engines, mostly 4-6-2Ts. In practice … engines were used more or less indiscriminately over all parts of the system. No.3 at Letterkenny on 23 June 1937 …eady to take out the evening train over the long trek to Burtonport. This line was closed in 1940, but owing to war …nditions part of it was reopened intermittently until 1947, when it finally closed down for ever.

The County Donegal Railway Joint Committee was an amalgamation in 1906 of four previously independent lines, of which the Strabane & Letterkenny still retained its nominal independence, together with the Strabane and Londonderry. This although worked by the County Donegal, was in fact owned after 1906 successively by the Midland Railway of England, the L.M.S., and for a short time British Railways. The ownership of the rest of the County Donegal Joint system was the rather curious one of the Great Northern of Ireland and the Midland (and in turn its successors). The total mileage of 3′ 0″ gauge was 124½ miles, the most extensive narrow gauge network in Ireland. Geographically the railway mainly served the southern part of County Donegal, and bore many resemblances to the Lough Swilly in the north, described in the previous chapter. This view shows a typical County Donegal steam train in later years, by which time most of the workings had been taken over by diesel railcars. These had been introduced in the early 1930s, the C.D. being an early pioneer in this form of passenger traffic operation. 2-6-4T No.2 *Blanche* (at Strabane, 20 April 1948) is now preserved in Belfast museum. The later locomotive stock consisted of two 4-4-4Ts, four 4-6-4Ts, and eight 2-6-4Ts. Previously there had been six 4-6-0Ts, all of which were out of service by 1931.

2-6-4T No.16 *Donegal* at Letterkenny in June 1937. Here the C.D.R.J.C. made contact with the Londonderry & Lough Swilly, and the Letterkenny & Burtonport Extension. In the background is one of the diesel railcars which, as already mentioned, latterly worked most of the services.

Londonderry, Victoria Road, one of the four terminal stations which this city once boasted. 2-6-4T No.6 *Columbkille* is leaving for Strabane, 20 April 1953. This L.M.S.-owned part of the system remained steam-worked until its closure in 1960. The figure on the left is the author, the photograph having been taken by his son.   [R. M. Casserley]

Two more 3′ 0″ gauge roadside tramways remain to be mentioned, the Clogher Valley Railway and the Castlederg & Victoria Bridge Tramway. The C.V.R., 37 miles long, ran between two connecting points on the G.N.R., at Tynan and Maguiresbridge, with its headquarters at Augnacloy, more or less midway between. The seven steam engines comprised six 0-4-2Ts and one 0-4-4T, examples of each being No.2 *Errigal* and No.7 *Blessingbourne* at Augnacloy on 18 September 1929. Latterly there was also a 2-6-2T from the C. & V.B.T.

No.6 *Erne* at Fivemiletown, the principal township on the line, with full station facilities, 25 June 1937.

No.6 again at the wayside halt of Stoneparkcross on the same day. The locomotive always ran bunker first, with the large headlight, providing useful illumination on the roadside sections. The line closed in 1942.

The C. & V.B.T. gave the small township of Castlederg connection with the G.N.R. main line at Victoria Bridge. This mixed train has just arrived at Castlederg on 7 April 1930, with 0-4-4T No.5. The other engines at the time were 2-6-0T No.4 and Beyer Peacock 2-4-0T No.6 from the N.C.C. of the well known Isle of Man type. On closure, the 2-6-0T went to the Clogher Valley, rebuilt as a 2-6-2T. This little tramway was an early casualty, having been closed in 1933.

O.V. Bulleid, the controversial locomotive designer, was one of the last advocates of steam, and held the post of C.M.E. on the Southern Railway in England at Nationalisation in 1948. At that date he went over to Ireland and took up a similar position on C.I.E. He had few opportunities to exercise his progressive ideas, but did manage to produce an engine remarkably similar to his ill-fated double-ended 0-6-6-0 'Leader' on the S.R., but designed to use turf instead of oil as was first intended. Various experiments had been made over the years to utilise Ireland's only natural fuel available in any worthwhile quantities, but for various reasons it had been found impracticable to burn it in a conventional locomotive firebox. Even so, with Bulleid's specially designed combustion arrangements it was not a success and in any event a programme of complete dieselisation was already under way. No.CC1—Bulleid's individuality again perpetuated the unique numbering scheme he had introduced on the S.R.—came out from Inchicore works in 1957, and ran about 2000 miles on trial. Little interest was taken after Bulleid's retirement in 1958 and so Ireland's last steam locomotive quietly faded away, something of an anti-climax after half a century of what may be regarded as the period of the 'Heyday of Steam'. This interesting machine was photographed lying out of use at Inchicore on 3 June 1961.

[R.M. Casserley]